How

10 Principles for Reclaiming Your Spirit

WRITINGS & DRAWINGS

ANGELA CAROLE BROWN

How the Light Gets In: 10 Principles for Reclaiming Your Spirit

H A I K U H O U S E

Some passages originally appeared in Angela's poetry collection *Bones* and her 100-word-story collection *Aleatory on the Radio*. Earlier versions of the principles and "in honor of the lowercase turning points" first appeared on her blog, Bindi Girl Chronicles.

Published by Haiku House
First Edition
ISBN-13: 978-1-7337453-4-5

Book Jacket Design & Interior Drawings by Angela Carole Brown.
(A color version of the pg 93 graphic was originally created by Angela for the book jacket of Stephen Long's *The Connectivity Principle*).
Author Photo is a video capture from the film *The Goddess Project* by Sara Landas & Holli Rae.

Angela Carole Brown is an author, poet, musician, and artist.
Visit the author at: **linktr.ee/angelacarolebrown**

HAIKU
HOUSE

2025

FOR P.

This book is dedicated with all my love and immense gratitude to my sister, who as early on in life as I can remember taught me about loving myself, having a voice, and using that voice. You've shattered my earth, in only the best ways.

FOREWORD

I first met Angela years ago when she attended a Wednesday evening meditation service I facilitated. I did not yet know she was an exceptional singer, writer, and visual artist. Over the years, a friendship developed as we walked each other through the joys and sometime struggles of life. We have literally spent time on the very trails she talks about in this book. Believe me when I say that Angela established her spiritual bonafides through the crucible of "having been there" and we are the beneficiaries of that Good Work!

In a world that seems increasingly unpredictable and full of challenges, finding a path to healing, wellness, and peace of mind can often feel like a daunting task. Yet, as we journey through life, it becomes clear that the true source of strength lies not in the external circumstances, but in the way we choose to engage with them. This little book offers a simple yet profound roadmap for navigating the tumult of life—a collection of ten principles and practices that I have found to be invaluable in my own journey of cultivating a life of balance and resilience.

With gentle encouragement vs. harsh directives, sharing rather than simply instructing, Angela nudges us to play with practices that are deep in their simplicity. These ten practices are not just mere suggestions—they are profoundly rooted in the spiritual understanding that our thoughts, beliefs, and actions shape our experience of reality. Each principle is a step toward a more harmonious existence, inviting us to live with intention and mindfulness. These practices are accessible to all, regardless of background or belief, and offer a gentle yet powerful guide to creating a life that reflects our highest potential.

Don't be surprised if you find yourself not just feeling a bit more connected and serene, but actually accessing creative energies held dormant by distraction—now bursting forth into expression. Enjoy the ride!

Rev. Michael McMorrow, D.D.
Granada Hills, California

A C K N O W L E D G M E N T S

For those who have been my wingspan on this path: Ajahn Ṭhānissaro Bhikkhu of the Metta Forest Monastery, Irma Breakfield, every one of the Browns in my immediate family (Afi, Andrew, Arman, Martha, Mike, Pam, Ted), Ellen Butterfield, Debbie Cole, Randy Fikki, Margo Gravelle, Fred Hicks, Carl Johnson, Chokae Kalekoa, Lily Knight, Michael McMorrow, Rose MG, Harmon Outlaw, Kelly Phillips, Kimberly Phillips, Stephen Rambo, Marilyn Roth, Eliasa Sabogal, Hans San Juan, Greg Stanton, Nikki Steen, Melanie Taylor, Chippewa Thomas, Lotus Weinstock, Barbara Wright, Arlene Zimmerly, Valerie Zoe, Center for Spiritual Living Granada Hills, Center for Spiritual Living Simi Valley, the Monday evening women's group, the Santa Clarita Saturday morning meet, Unity of Pasadena, and Unity Southeast in Kansas City.

Beloveds, I am eternally grateful for your kinship and for your impact on the spiritual transformation and wellness constantly unfolding in my life.

love + more love
acb

How the Light Gets In

10 Principles for Reclaiming Your Spirit

This night shall pass.
Then we have work to do.
Everything has to do with
loving and not loving.

RUMI

The birds they sang
at the break of day.
Start again
I heard them say.
Don't dwell
on what has passed away
or what is yet to be …
Ring the bells that still can ring.
Forget your perfect offering.
There is a crack in everything,
that's how the light gets in.

LEONARD COHEN

CONTENTS

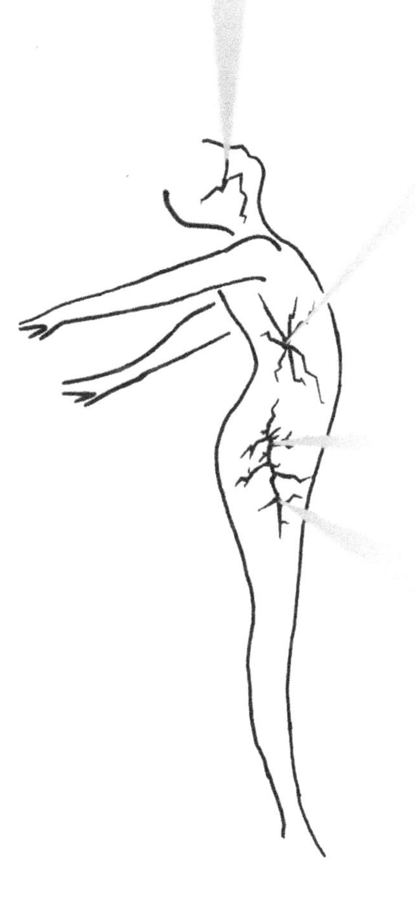

in

honor

of the

lowercase

turning points

These are astonishing times. And I have felt led to put pen to paper, and to share my personal offering on emotional wellness, yet I can't imagine anything inspiring Imposter Syndrome faster than daring to write a wellness book. Who am I to dispense any kind of suggestions for inner work, self-care, and transformational healing when I'm, as often as anyone, faced with my own fair amount of struggle? Yes, friends, that's the question that has beaned me in the head several times throughout this process. Until one day it hit me … this is all of us. It's Deepak and Brené and Jane Doe and Joe Blow. We're all primed to testify to our own experiences and epiphanies precisely because we're human and by definition have tussled with uncertainty, pain, and trauma.

What I do know for sure, as these troubling times unfold, is that we must take care of our spirits. And so, this little book is about what we can do to better ourselves for the challenges ahead and the ones already here. Self-care has been a popular catchphrase for a while now but is often misunderstood. It is more than spa massages and bubble baths, and is not remotely the posterchild for privileged self-indulgence that some claim. Self-care is healing from within the hurting parts that keep us from being our best toward each other and ourselves.

So, here I am. A willing and imperfect student, on a path of wellness and spiritual transformation. I'd started to type "on a path *to* wellness and spiritual transformation" and something stopped me. I'm not walking toward anything. As I suspect is the case for us all, I'm already in it, deeply steeped.

Already inside of wellness and transformation as an ever-evolving, ever-churning call to revolutionary action. And I say revolutionary because in today's American culture, what's most important, what's most revered, are ambition and relentless drive. There have even been television shows that have pitted twelve-year-olds against each other in competition to inspire the shark in them. How did we become this? So, to choose a path of wellness, radical self-care, and rest, over celebrating exhaustion and the edict to *produce! produce! produce!* ... IS revolutionary.

For each of us the path looks different, and all roads truly do lead to Rome. For me, the soul's journey began decades ago, when I found myself floundering. I was in a relationship (perhaps even a life) that wasn't working, brawling with depression, and feeling stuck. And my dear friend, the late great comedian/sage Lotus Weinstock, asked me: *"What's it gonna be, Angela, wellness or illness?"* It was a question that has never left me. The inference, of course, was ... if you're not fostering the one, by default you're fostering the other.

It was the mightiest call to action because it scared me. It also reminded me of Martin Luther King Jr's espousal that the highest form of maturity is self-inquiry, which has always resonated with me. So, between these two potent prompts began a practice of turning inward, self-examining, and then acting.

The soul's journey, investigative to its core, has had my lifetime membership in a myriad of nourishing ways ever since, both as a personal practice and as creative expression: From studying the principles of Buddhism, Taoism, metaphysics & New Thought, working with archetypal symbology through an intuitive discipline by Seena Frost called SoulCollage®, deep diving into kundalini yoga, and, newest on this journey, two potent & powerful 12-Step programs of recovery … to having sung with a Vedic kirtan chant ensemble for a glorious spell, producing yoga and meditation CDs, making little moviettes like my documentary short in search of connections called *The Sanctuary Project* and my short feature for children on gratitude called

The Richest Girl in the World. All these modalities have changed me in ways unquantifiable. Even the creative works, put out expressly for the public's experience, are often my loving guides through moments of chaos and delusion.

Case in point: I've made my life in the arts, and what can tend to come with the artist's life is a kind of existential pursuit of authenticity and recognition (*"If no one sees it, does it even exist? Do I even exist?"*), accompanied by an arbitrary vision of an arrival point that once achieved can then be called a success. So, for me, there was always this abstract sense of the singular Big Break that I was perpetually chasing.

One thing turning inward has illuminated for me is that life is a series of beautiful unfoldments. A seed is planted. It flowers. It dies. It goes back to seed. It repeats. We unfold. We bloom in consciousness. We make mistakes, sometimes grave ones, and the cracks and fissures show up. We learn something from the cracks if we're willing and wholehearted, which begins the process of an old consciousness dying and a rebirth occurring. And if we're not willing, that's when we suffer. It's a wild, messy, dark, bright, challenging, effortless, one step forward, two steps back, magnificent, clumsy ride. And the all-uppercase GIANT TURNING POINT is a leprechaun.

How it actually happens is the hundreds of thousands of daily, micro, precious, lowercase turning points that, one by one, profoundly shape us into who we most authentically are. On the occasions I'm able to recognize such serendipities, it is in those moments that I smile so wide I can't contain myself and am reminded that I am here to art for art's sake. And when I don't recognize them, because I'm being tone-deaf or governed by my pain, I'm at least learning to surrender my absolute knowing that they're happening anyway, running my engine for me when I'm feeling too broken or unconscious to. The idea even inspired a haiku.

life is beautiful
bringing up the rear for me
till I get it right

Perhaps that very surrender is God. Infinite Intelligence. Source. A million names and a million definitions for a grand mystery that is, frankly, beyond language and beyond human linear thought, yet keeps me always betting on the good.

Today, the idea of chasing anything has become tired and dusty for me. What seems to be replacing it is recognizing my inherent worth and holding space for what is actually meant for me in this life. It may not, after all, look like what I've always envisioned.

Just. Stay. Open. I have to remind myself of this, honor this, and practice this every single day. When I do, I am happiest. When I'm in my frustrations, I know why.

The same concept follows work of the soul, which is what I've chosen to help navigate mental and spiritual wellness in my life. The *aha!* twist is that we have to choose soul work again and again every single day. It isn't a choose-once, learn-something-powerful, and never-struggle-again deal.

There's no finite arrival of enlightenment. It's not static. Spiritual transformation is a movable, pliable, living, breathing animal precisely because new areas of development continually emerge. But small steps every day, as beneficial to daily life as eating and sleeping, can help keep us attuned and resonating on that higher frequency.

And the beauty in tripping? A magical word indeed ... *reset*. And magical, because there is no failure here, only getting up and getting up again, as often as needed.

Helping me with this are 10 principles I have discovered experientially as direct pathways for reclaiming a spirit that at times can get buried under life's stresses. I credit for this discovery the many soul-tending modalities mentioned earlier, but I also, quite frankly, credit the pandemic that landed on us all in 2020. Both have been the very conduits for these principles to be able to alchemize into a kind of spiritual algorithm in my life.

Today, I'd like to share them with you.

Taking a cue from poet/musician/shaman Leonard Cohen, these practices don't so much seal the cracks — in some kind of presumption that the cracks are inherently broken and need fixing — as they use those very cracks *AS* the brilliant vehicles for the light to get in.[1]

And because these are anxious and concerning times for democracy and for the very basics of compassionate humanity, maybe it's also a matter of how the light gets out … and thus, given to the world.

Navigating the murky waters of life is a job with tenure. All the money and station in the world won't reprieve us from the task. As Rumi says, *"we have work to do."*[2] And so, I present to you now my spiritual algorithm, 10 small but mighty principles that can mean the difference between the grind of life and truly living. Costs nothing. Big Pharma has no equity in THIS medicine.

Yikes!

ONE

turn away

from anxiety-

fueling

news

programs

Just refuse them. They litter television and the internet and are designed for one agenda only — to whip us into a distracted frenzy by increasing our anxiety and stress, and by virtue weaken us and our pocketbooks at the seams. Because having an entire culture in panic mode is profitable and never about being in the public's interest. Thanks to social media, any outlet can call itself news. Sites that create sensationalist headlines for the express purpose of profit-generating clickbait do not have journalism or the public's best interest as their motive. They produce non-stories that have nothing to do with information-dispensing and everything to do with gossip-mongering, disinformation, and shock value. They are specifically designed to appeal to our limbic brain instincts.

Information is valuable. Hysteria never is. So tread vigilantly. Find your news through legitimate sources. Some say the printed form can tend less toward superficial soundbites, hyperbole, and slant, as print has the burden of process rather than the knee-jerkness of insta-posting.

Do the homework needed to figure out who and what is delivering the highest value content. In today's reality, that may not be as easy as it should be in a free society, as even time-honored fourth estate institutions are suddenly experiencing the flog of intimidation, if not the outright obstruction of access and reportage. Yet we must not waver in championing those who honorably deliver to us what is happening in the world.

And even when you do find the news you need, recognize when your precious nervous system needs a break from the onslaught of overstimulation in this information age where our phones are perpetually propped in our back pockets. Staying informed about the human family and the wide, wide world in which it lives is important. But it's equally important to take a break, rejuvenate, cleanse the palate, and tune back in when you've freed up some disk space.

Do not allow others to shame you into being a news junkie, glued to bulletins round the clock, wrestling with a constant cell-decaying "fight, flight, or freeze" mode leading to chronic stress, and spiraling in a compulsive loop of doom-scrolling. Make sanity and serenity your priority. Choose quality over quantity.

Oooooooooooh!

TWO

read

for

pleasure

Those who read books travel the world and time itself. Are explorers, adventurers, discoverers. Take on beggars and kings with no thought in the ranking. Have their minds forced open and their spirits ever expanding in insatiable hunger for more. Those who read books fill themselves with wonder. Know that a book is a friend, a teacher, a priest, an agitator. Are not afraid to be made uncomfortable. Grow the wings that continue, muscle by muscle, to sprout upon reaching "The End" time and time anew. Fly. Fall. Fly again. Those who read books are changed. And glad of it.

Clearly, I'm a lover of books.

As a writer, I want to encourage books. I want to encourage good books. I want to encourage literature. But hey, read a magazine. Just read. For pure enjoyment and entertainment. And try as often as possible to do it outside the digital and electronic universe. E-books are convenient space-savers and great for travel, but don't let them be your exclusive source for reading. The brain needs a good chunk of quality time every day removed from electromagnetic energy, and to be reminded of the world of imagination and connection that does exist beyond our digital screens.

As a very young child, before I could read, I loved listening to stories on the family record player. *Peter and the Wolf* and a beloved collection of Czechoslovakian folktales narrated by Danny Kaye were the pinnacles of that experience for me, because they expanded the very notion of a whole world beyond my tiny hamlet of Compton, California.

I was so enchanted to travel journeys with the heroes and sheroes of these tales, and to get into adventures with them. Even at four years old, certain passages stuck in my little head from obsessive listenings, and I would perform them for my family. And a performer was born. But a lover of stories was also born. I couldn't wait to learn to read, because I was promised by my book-loving parents that many more stories awaited me there.

It can be tough to carve time for pleasure reading. Sometimes tougher than we even understand. It wasn't until about a year ago that I realized I hadn't completed reading a book since … well … I had to really think back. I would always start one, and eventually abandon it. And when I made myself think back on how long it had been, I realized that a kind of paralysis had struck, and it coincided with Covid lockdown. I'd always instinctively known that trauma was a genuine reality for us during that time, and I hadn't even recognized one of the ways in which it had manifested in me. I had started grieving that I'd lost my love for reading. But I hadn't. I'd experienced trauma. And once I could identify that, I was able to take gentle steps to rebuild that muscle. Now I'm gleefully returning, and I can't adequately explain just what books do for my soul, my serenity, my critical thinking, the expansion of my intellectual and empathic scope, and how different all of that had looked on me during those four paralytic years. Reading books has been my salvation.

And while we're on the subject, and inside this principle, I would be remiss if I didn't acknowledge the giant White Rabbit, Anansi the Spider, and Horton the Elephant in the room. In addition to whatever your reading pleasures are, from my deepest heart this plea. Go find and read banned books. Pass them on to others. Help keep books and public libraries alive for the continued free flow of information. If they are that threatening to a particular system, question the system not the books.

They remain the greatest gift my parents ever gave me. Experiencing beautiful, devastating, buoyant stories, and exhilarating language, this custom gives me life.

For my fellow book lovers, you already know. If you're not much of one, take the leap and see for yourself what soul-filling adventures await.

And not for nothin' … but reading also slows your heart rate.

Ommmmmmm

THREE

meditate

… or at the very least find a way to be in the silence and stillness for a few minutes every day … which is really all meditation is — an opportunity for intentional breathing and to be at rest. The more minutes you can find in that stillness, the better able you'll be to heed the still small voice. Consider a wonderful memoir by Sara Maitland[3] on her experiment of withdrawing from the world for a period, in pursuit of silence. There is a wealth of discussion to be had on the topic and its impact on a society, and which is utterly compelling. For now, for this, simply allow yourself a few minutes each day to power everything down. Your nervous system will thank you.

This specific suggestion is not to diminish the power and wonder of guided meditations, chant & mantra meditations, labyrinth meditations, zen/ambient music & sound bath meditations. The varieties are endless and rich like golden soil. And especially for those who are naturally restless, supplement meditations can be incredibly helpful in attuning your consciousness to a specific focus. But at the end of the day, some amount of simple silence and stillness (as much as we ever have any control over our environment) and conscious breathing, also known as prānayama, will truly feed the all-important "rest & digest" parasympathetic nervous system, restore and maintain homeostasis, lessen the monkey mind chatter, calm the bellows of anger, aid depression, and allow you to be a receiver instead of a perpetual searcher.

If you're a newbie at this, start with one minute and build from there. Set a timer if it helps. And though these have a very meaningful place in yogic rituals, there's absolutely no obligation here to sit in lotus position or to place your hands in gyan mudra. Just make yourself comfortable in whichever way works for you.

It's a simple prescription, really, and a sort-of cousin to Vipassanā meditation: Sit. Be still. Close your eyes. Breathe in. Breathe out. Notice every wandery thought, every breath, every sound, every physical sensation. Accept each notice without judgment, but merely as witness. When judgment comes — and it will, we're beautifully human — notice that too. Repeat.

There's no need to goal for anything. You are right where you need to be for this.

The action is small. The impact … immense.

awakening

FOUR

connect

with

higher

power

The scope and breadth of this ubiquitous noun phrase is as expansive as the oceans, so even the most ardent atheist can identify theirs. Something that is quite simply greater than your prosaic self and has guidance and insight to offer you, feed you, challenge you, and minister to your psyche and soul.

Maybe it's the collective unconscious. Maybe it's your own higher consciousness, which exists in every human, usually buried beneath all the layers of trauma and dysfunction, but there, just ripe and ready to coach us, if we're keen to do some excavating. Maybe it's nature. Maybe it's the source within. Or a source out there. Maybe it's the wisdom of hindsight contained within the bosom of the ancestors. Maybe it's simply the concept of goodness.

Or maybe Lao Tzu had it right when he said that the minute you think you've got a handle on this all-encompassing, mysterious lifeforce, you've lost it. So, free yourself from the obligation.

And because it is a profoundly personal relationship or co-creatorship, it will show up differently for every individual on the planet. Usually when we're quieting the monkey mind chatter in our heads and are open to receiving. Yet it is that unquantifiable *something* that operates as capital C Counsel, crucially anchors us in a temper of essential humility, maneuvers us around the landmines, and connects us to each other. There is no need to affix a label, or to name it. Simply be with it. Find yours. Plug in regularly. And listen.

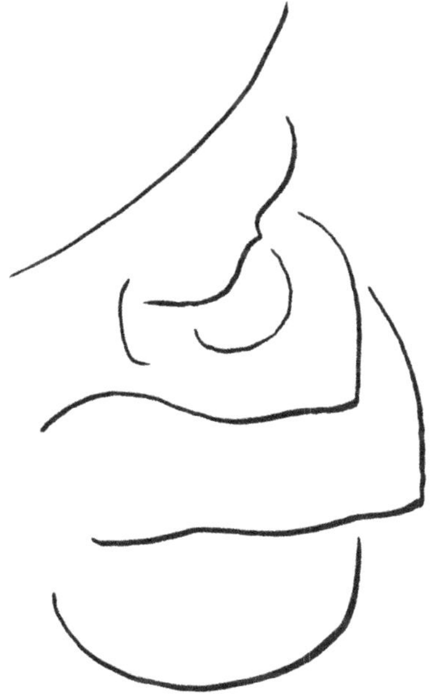

Creation

FIVE

create

even if you

don't consider

yourself an artist

"Artist" is just a label. We all have creativity and imagination within us, and it can often show up in the most unexpected cloak, which is usually how it works anyway. Create *THINGS*. Conjure *IDEAS*. Make messy art without limits or rules. Feed it. Allow it to feed you. Have fun with it. In times both light and dark, the benefits to soul are untold.

When March of 2020 happened to the world, and we went into global pandemic lockdown, I and my best friend and her two teens, with whom I was living during that strange and unsettling time, decided to spruce up our nightly dinners with something playful. It was the only way we could find to keep ourselves sane. Especially the kids, who were climbing the walls, unable to see their friends, go to school, do life as they knew life to be. My best friend and I, much older than the teens, experienced a combination of that same upheaval AND a wee bit of recognizing the blessing in being forced to slow down.

Still, we all needed a mode for sanity and anchor, and the kids came up with the brilliant idea of doing dinner each night with a different theme, which would be announced at the beginning of our day. We would then each, with whatever resources we had in our closets, come to dinner dressed in the given theme.

Ideas were everything from *Star Wars*, *The Matrix*, the decade of the nineteen-eighties (which was hilarious legend to the kids), the TV show *Parks and Recreation*, and on and on. Come dinner time, we'd get the food ready, set the table, then disappear into our bedrooms and meet back at the table to reveal our cosplay.

On eighties night, I dressed as an aerobics teacher, complete with Jheri curl wig, off-the-shoulder sweatshirt, headband, and leg warmers. And someone else among us came to dinner as Flavor Flav. We fell out in uncontrollable laughter, applauding each others' efforts, one more inventive than the next, and then commenced with enjoying our meal. For those first upheaved months, this was our nightly ritual.

In a global cataclysm where laughter can be as elusive as gold dust, with loss and uncertainty all around, this was an equally silly *and* mightily restorative ritual. Hey, Oak Vale Four, we done good!

That is the power of creativity in action.

bliss

SIX

play

&

rest

First off, let yourself be a child again. An idea very closely linked to the previous principle, and which is not the same as being child-ISH.

There is so much management, planning, and fortune-making that has governed our adult lives that we can easily allow it to collapse our spirits. Easy to get so caught up in *building* our lives that we can forget to actually *live* our lives. I have been more guilty in this area than a lot.

Hearkening once again back to 2020, as an entire globe quarantined, the mandated stay-at-home orders forced us to slow down whether we wanted to or not. As a result, some truly profound epiphanies were had from the many about the lives we'd been living before the pandemic.

And though we were locked down, connections were still able to be forged, because we as a culture were industrious in finding ways to maintain our sanity through recreation. For nearly a year spent in the state of severance, the many threw Zoom parties, staged social distancing drive-by parades, live-streamed living room performances and solo kitchen concerts (a wealth of that among my beloved musician community provided a daily, soul-filling scroll through Facebook and Instagram), and of course played dress-up to come to the dinner table. 😉

The ideas were endless because they woke up our Inner Child. We literally relearned, while surrounded by illness and disruption, how to *go to recess* and find our needed respite in playing fiercely and making connections with each other, because that life force is simply unshakable.

The flip side of that same spirit is to rest. And just to bring it home, this reminder: As important as a good work ethic is, neither of these prompts is about work. Plenty of that is instilled in us our whole lives. The Italians have a delicious term for the temperament of resting — *dolce far niente* — literally translated as the "sweetness of doing nothing." They have raised it to an art, yet in our ambition-worshipping American culture we have stapled the label of shame to it. We do not need to be in the constant state of mergers and acquisitions. Because of the pandemic, we were in collective trauma. I believe many are again. There should never be shame attached to *not* being okay. On the contrary, there should be precious time carved to take care of not being okay. And even when we are, we'll have a better shot at staying that way if we can honor the balance of motion and rest.

So, regardless of what is going on in the world, and there is plenty right now that would stupefy the stoic, take the pressure off when you feel the call. Listen to the stress signals of your mind, body, and spirit. Nap. Daydream. Watch movies. Binge your favorite series. Read a book with a fragrant cup of tea, or a rich dark roast. Take long walks. Stroll museums. Frolic and play. Sit and gaze in cafés with no agenda. Rest. Restore. Renew. It is the essential yin to our Everest-conquering yang.

blossoming

SEVEN

commune

with

nature

Now, honestly, I don't think any further word on this one is even necessary. It's kind of self-selling. Except that I'm compelled to share what happened to me roughly ten years ago, because in some ways it seems to be the mother lode for me. I never truly got the phrase "commune with nature" — that spiritual directive, as I now view it — until I began the ritual for myself. Out of the blue, it seemed, I started hankering for some wildlands. And I think, at least in part, it was because I'd been a meditator for a good many years already, yet ten years ago I began growing intermittently flustered by the struggle to truly burrow deep with my practice, and my belief that it had to do with the inability to remove myself from the world's distractions.

One truth about meditation is that doing it is possible even if the sky is falling all around us, but that's some pretty hardcore level of meditation badassery that I have never achieved. I need an environment that allows moving out of the world for a small chunk of time as often as I can. Enter nature.

At that time ten years ago, I was blessed to be living in a community that smacked right up against a set of glorious mountain ranges, the ever sprawling and resilient Angeles National Forest in Southern California and its various canyons and waterfalls. That said, I don't believe there exists a community that has zero access to some brand of nature. A mountain, an ocean, a lake, even a park or community garden. We can all find some.

Now, me? I hike my nature. But you may find your richest experience with it by whipping out your green thumb to till some earth and sow some seeds. You may score yourself beneficial negative ions from placing bare feet right in the soil or lying on grass. Sitting on sand and staring out at an ocean is unbelievably peaceful. Endless, creative, and inclusive are the ways to experience nature. Even the incarcerated are given time outside to breathe vital fresh air.

The particular SoCal canyon I started hiking, at the northern end of Los Angeles County, is part crest, overlooking wide sweeps of mountain, part enchanted forest, taking one into the bowels of nature with groves of trees bridging overhead and creating a canopy. What I never saw coming was the way in which this daily ritual would become something I would crave the way one craves coffee.

Runners talk about the runner's high. Gym nuts are antsy if they miss a day of working out. That has never been me. But

I started craving this. And I found that not only did it aid me in getting more oxygen into my life and lungs, slowing my heart rate, and increasing my digestive juices, but it also worked as the meditative tool I'd been looking for, shifting my entire sense of mental wellness, and, most profoundly, most surprisingly, opening my heart chakra in ways I couldn't have predicted.

Communing with critters beyond my cat and other humans. Listening to their concert. Okay, encountering the odd snake here and there was a bit of a challenge for this ol' phobe, but I learned to navigate them with a modicum of harmony. Moving among the wise old trees (check out Hermann Hesse sometime on trees … *my god*).[4] Recognizing the cruciality of taking care of the earth. And truly understanding the dire consequences of continuing as we are, in promoting carbon footprinting and the decimation of the ozone. These were the peaceful experiences *and* sobering contemplations I was having on the daily as I walked this nature. And it told me in no uncertain terms that my heart was indeed opening.

I'm still at it today, ten years later, although with more challenges where I recently moved to whenever the snowy months arrive. But I try not to let the ritual hibernate for long, because it's been an experience that has made me live in gratitude for what I have, and where I am in life, and what is precious. The Tao Te Ching teaches us to be in harmony with nature (even snakes :/). For certain, nature brings me to a peaceable place whenever life is throwing roadblocks my way.

It has also shifted my worthiness mechanism. Today I feel more open to receiving blessings. And, in fact, I am developing the ability to see just how blessings are flying all around us like gnats, and are already in everything that happens to us. Not only that which feels good, and is about comfort and prosperity, and is easy to see as a blessing, but even the stuff, or people, we consider toxic because they are what serve as lessons, opportunities, and teachers. And that may actually be where the real gold lies.

It's ours to choose to recognize, or not. And I do understand that sometimes it's simply easier on our constantly tested comfort zones to clamp down instead, bear the armor of hurt, perhaps even indulge a bit in the quiet awe of others, because maybe we have no real clue who we are without our wounds. In that regard, it does take a certain amount of stepping forward into a daunting unknown to keep our hearts open. But it is worth the leap. Because keeping our hearts open is the greatest kind of surgery our bodies can undergo. And being in nature is most remarkable at opening up that mighty vessel for our daily access.

Love

EIGHT

forgive

(& ask

forgiveness)

Question:
What if the person who's harmed me doesn't deserve forgiveness?

Answer:
Forgive anyway.

Because the forgiveness is not about them. In an ideal universe, my forgiveness would move heaven and earth in them. Change them where they stand. Tremble the earth beneath their feet. I rather like thinking I have that kind of magnetism and sway. But when have we ever lived in an ideal universe? And when are we ever that Jesus-like? The truth is, people only truly change because they are compelled to, because something has trembled the earth under their feet, and not because of any magical touch from us and our magnanimous generosity of spirit.

Which isn't to say our example can't inspire others. Of course it can. Especially if we're living from our higher vibration. Ultimately, however, the decision to make a change because of someone else's example is a deeply inside job. Neither you nor I can pressure that change out of anyone.

Years in a rigorous Al-Anon program, as well as personal experience with it, has taught me this. So, it can't be the reason behind choosing to forgive. The reason for forgiving is because carrying grudges is corrosive, deteriorating us on the cellular level. It is a burden too great. And it is absolutely within our agency to do something about that tonnage.

Somewhere I read that forgiveness is giving up the hope of a better yesterday. And as a Champion Grudge Holder, who is in recovery and works to maintain true reformation every day, I can personally vouch for the darkness that shrouded me for years over a couple of deep hurts I simply could not forgive. When I say these went on for decades, that is not hyperbole. And they served me *not one bit*. Well … there WAS that ol' righteous superiority of The Wound (she confesses, shaking head). But today, that is not the part of me I want served.

What made me finally give over, frankly, was simple exhaustion. That was one freaking heavy boulder of self-righteousness to carry on my back. And once I decided that it crippled more than lifted me, and I was able to *expect nothing* in return for my forgiveness to each of these persons in my life, the shift in me and my sense of happiness and serenity was truly confounding. AND both of these people ended up back in my life in very positive ways. Because they were no longer the people who had hurt me. Neither even sought my forgiveness, as I'm not sure either ever realized the gravity of the hurt they'd caused. Either that, or I conjured a pair of epic wounds out of thin air that suffocated me for decades. And none of that mattered. I had finally unburdened my heart by forgiving.

But what if they *are* still the same folks who hurt us? And are capable of further hurt? And we have absolutely no interest in forgiving? If anything, we feel mighty royal wearing that grudge like a crown.

Those examples are also in my life. People I do my best to send love and light whenever I think on them, and genuinely wish health and wellness in their lives, while knowing unequivocally that they cannot come back into mine, because that toxicity still persisted the last time I knew anything, and I am finally learning the importance of setting boundaries.

If the only thing that your authentic forgiveness accomplishes is allowing you to let such a person's grip on you release, and with it all that heavy weight of hurt, and with it all that power you handed over to them on a satin pillow, *your* power in *their* hands (think on that one a minute), you will have achieved the one thing that truly matters. You will have begun to lighten that load, and for it heal your spirit from the inside out.

So, how do we do that? Forgive when our hearts aren't ready? When anger and hurt still course through us?

Ask for the willingness. Ask for help in putting down your sword. If you're a pray-er, then that part's easy. If you're not, consider asking anyway. Out loud. To the ether. Quantum physics says that what we put out into the energetic field gets received and influences matter. If you don't swallow that one either, then just consider the asking to be an attunement of your own consciousness. Even just *considering* the possibility that earnest forgiveness does heal us, by asking for the willingness out loud, perhaps making it a mantra for yourself, you might just be nudged into greatly benefitting from the assignment and its accompanying shift. My experience tells me to always opt for the shift.

And perhaps the hardest forgiveness to willingly proffer is the one we may owe to ourselves. I think it's safe to say that many of us can sometimes speak to the mirror in ways we'd never speak to anyone else. And maybe it's because we view it as a bit of tough love administered to make us straighten out a worrisome bend. Or, even more concerning, perhaps we feel undeserving of kinder treatment. Self-love can be hard-won if we're battling with stresses that would benefit from professional counseling. Just know that over time self-disparagement will degrade a spirit that — without argument — deserves better. We do deserve better. We know it even when we don't know it. Granted, that's a statement that fully bets on the existence of a vibrational Lower and Higher Self in each of us.

Because even if the perhaps odd paradigm of Lower You asking forgiveness, and Higher You granting it, is inherently meta and seems silly, what I do know for myself is that this action is an invaluable opportunity to practice gentleness toward the only ME that I'll have in this lifetime. And that's not a small thing.

Likewise, asking the forgiveness of another. In the 12 Steps of Recovery it is the 9th Step, and it regards making amends. There is no greater burden to unload, no greater liberation when unburdened, than being accountable for a behavior, for having hurt someone, even unintentionally, but especially intentionally, and making an earnest vow to that someone to do and to be better.

Here's the key, though. When we ask such forgiveness, we have to be prepared for "no." It doesn't happen often, as people usually appreciate a gesture of earnest humility that doesn't include excuses for the behavior. And how wonderful when it can genuinely heal a relationship. But "no" *can* happen, and the crucial thing to remember is that the outcome of your apology and amends is not up to you. You cannot control the narrative. Only your part in the play.

That's it. That's all. And I pray that doesn't come off as flippant, because that's actually a tough one for me. I want to control everything in my environment. Entire anxiety disorders have been birthed from my need to control my environment, and the futility in the try.

When I'm asking forgiveness, I must remind myself vigilantly that the narrative isn't mine to control, and that what will always be more compelling is the lessening of that two-ton forged steel wrecking ball and the lightening of my spirit.

And yes, I've been there too. Making an amends to someone who would not receive it. I have to live with that. But whenever that person crosses my mind, there is an immediate sting of humility in the reminder that I am human and flawed, and that there was a consequence to my behavior. And I choose to lean into that rather than try to shake it off, because being humbled is never a bad thing. The bottom line is that with my amends, my soul was righted because ultimately I did the right thing. The rest is out of my hands.

The other bottom line (in this mutant, double-bottomed universe) is that we don't need the whole world to fall in step with our agenda of happiness in order to cultivate it for ourselves. That too is a purely inside job. It isn't always an easy shift to make, but there *is* great power in letting that notion go.

When we ask forgiveness, and when we earnestly forgive, regardless of outcomes beyond our control, we accomplish an uptick in integrity, and an unburdening of the soul like no other.

That alone is vital medicine.

blessed

NINE

honor

a daily

gratitude

ritual

As someone in two 12-Step programs and therefore intimately familiar with the nightly 10th Step of inventorying my day and delivering it to my sponsor, the discovery of a gratitude ritual has been a gamechanger for me. I don't think the power of gratitude can be overestimated. Even on the days when I'm feeling so blah that all I can think to jot down is *"I'm grateful I woke up"* as though there is literally nothing else good that's happened, that single acknowledgment is casting something mightily high-octane into the ether, by framing my life by what I have versus what I don't. And that shift is palpable.

In all honesty, most days I have no trouble finding things to be grateful for. It continually astonishes me just how much that tiny shift in consciousness can remind me how blessed my life actually is … right when I'm feeling neglected by it. Michael Beckwith's jewel, *"you cannot bring anything new into your life until you're grateful for what you have now,"*[5] for me, speaks profoundly to the misconceptions of lack.

Of course, you don't have to be in a 12-Step program to have a gratitude ritual. That's just where I found mine. And such a practice can be in any form: a list, a journal log, a mantra, a meditation, a prayer. I once heard someone say that prayer needn't ever be anything more than two words … *thank you.* Just one idea to consider.

A tradition I've recently been finding great beauty in is blessing my food. We always said blessing at my parents' dinner table in childhood. Somehow, it got associated in my brain with being an old-fashioned tradition, because I just completely dropped it from my life once I became an adult. I also didn't know a single person who still blessed their meals. But as I've become more attuned with the idea, I've suddenly discovered quite a few folks who still do. Funny how that works.

And what a lovely idea to express out loud our thankfulness for the bounty on our plates, and for not taking a meal for granted but cherishing it for what it gives us, especially considering how many don't have that luxury. Personally, as someone whose other program of recovery is for disordered eating, I find blessing my meals to be unbelievably powerful in helping me to reframe my food in the proper way. Not as enemy or drug, punishment or reward, but as sacred and privileged sustenance that gives my body what it needs to flourish.

Now, imagine employing that same gratitude practice with everything. Just imagine.

And lastly …

family

TEN

be

of

service

When the pandemic came calling and lockdown was a nearly yearlong mandate, the displays of altruism were incredibly moving to me. People came together on Zoom meets to organize and deliver to their communities what was needed. From sewing and dispensing face masks to surprise drop-offs of groceries at someone's door, to making food kits for people in need, to outreach calls, the pandemic showed us what we're made of and that it wasn't only the frontliners who could be of help. We all had the ability to be there for others, whether for an individual or a community at large.

I'm reminded of the Henry James quote: *"Happiness, we are told, is accomplished by getting out of oneself. The point, however, is not only to get out but to stay out. And in order to do that, one must have a compelling errand."*[6]

Service may just be the most compelling errand there is, and certainly the most restorative unguent for self-absorption if that happens to be your struggle. Maybe you don't struggle with it. I certainly do when I'm not in the work. Hence, it's just one of the tangles I am healing gently, one knot at a time, and with attendant love.

Whether we're struggling with it or not, the idea of being on the planet and in this life to serve our fellow humans is startlingly beautiful. In my own struggles with self-absorption, one thing I truly believed was that if I gave any amount of my time, my involvement, or my money to someone else in need, my own needs would not be met, because I only had so much mental bandwidth left over at the end of any given day, never mind the actual and literal limitations of my time and money. I was operating from my scared reptilian brain. And because I chose a path in this life that means I'll likely be working a job until I drop, the necessity for self-absorption was always an easy case to plead, as in: *I need to take care of ME. I have nothing left to give anybody else.*

I began my most earnest path to service in my first program of recovery, where we are continually encouraged to pass on what we've learned to fellow sufferers. One way specifically in 12-Step is by being a sponsor. I'm pretty sure I remember kicking and screaming, trying to jut my foot against the doorsill of that particular threshold. I believed there was no room in my recovery for others. Yet once I was finally brave enough to take the leap, not only did I learn just how much it has *not* taken a single thing away from my life, but I discovered and continue to experience just how much it gives … and gives … and gives … full bore to my life.

As 12-Step readies me always to be a more giving version of myself, not only within the confines of recovery but also out into the larger world (*"... to practice these principles in all our affairs"*),[7] I find myself thinking about Rumi's words: *"Everything has to do with loving and not loving."*[8] Yes. Everything. It all comes down to this simple quotient.

I believe it's no accident my finding the spiritual center that today I call home. There are, for the record, two other dear-to-my-heart centers I will always call home, but this here is about my present condition. Found merely by Googling "New Thought centers" when I relocated from Los Angeles to the Midwest halfway through Covid lockdown, Unity Southeast in Kansas City was the only New Thought I could find open at the time. Known for its ministry of community service, especially regarding a houseless population that didn't stop needing help just because a pandemic had arrived, Unity practiced every safety precaution while continuing to offer overnight bedding accommodations in the winter months, and massive monthly grocery giveaways year-round. They weren't about to abandon their constituency-in-need. And that moved me deeply.

Being perfectly base, I chose Unity Southeast because it was open — plain and simple. Being a child of grace, it chose *me* because service was a consciousness I needed.

And especially as we all try to find meaning in a world that lately seems senseless and cruel, I will stake my life on saying that service, and being a good steward of the earth and of the human family, is the single most potent go-to for recovering or establishing one's spirit as a person of value on the planet …

and within.

in

honor

of

radiant

you

So, there you have it, friends. 10 accessible principles from which I get immense help toward this ongoing cultivation of healing, wellness, and footing in an unstable world.

To briefly recap:

1 – turn away from anxiety-fueling news programs
2 – read for pleasure
3 – meditate
4 – connect with higher power
5 – create even if you don't consider yourself an artist
6 – play & rest
7 – commune with nature
8 – forgive (& ask forgiveness)
9 – honor a daily gratitude ritual
10 – be of service

This 10-pt prescription for wellness never supposes to replace professional therapeutic services that are for persistent psychological issues. A suggested soul nourishment practice purely — that we can do ourselves, at home, in our lives, simple moves and pivots in consciousness — is the pledge of this little book. And I thank you for reading it.

So, how does any of this apply to the world we're facing right now? On our best days, we want our spiritual and mental wellness to be strong and practiced … so that on our most challenging, we are better able to face and respond to the threats on humanity in ways that still allow us to own our happiness. Which isn't measured by external factors but by how well we are living in our integrity.

I am a New Year baby, so it's in my DNA to seek rituals. To chant, to pray, to dance, to give auspiciousness to new beginnings and rites of passage. To participate in burning bowl rituals and labyrinth walks, to summon the rains and the gods, to howl at the moon, to burn sage, build altars, close my eyes, shut off the valves, and listen. Listen to the wind in the trees tell me what I need to know next, what I need to do next, how I need to sing next. And then I sing.

I hope you'll sing too. Continue unfolding. Bloom in brilliant consciousness. Grow your spirit the breadth of the skies and the depths of your loveliest dreams.

To radiant you, I offer this Metta Prayer of Lovingkindness:

May you always be filled with wonder in recognizing the hundreds of lowercase turning points swirling about you. A glorious baptism of blessings.

May you maintain the daily fostering of wholeness and serenity, untethered laughter, and a vibrant, pulsating, life force.

May you give yourself some ease today and live by the song-smith's words: *Forget your perfect offering.*[9]

May you cherish your lifegiving prāna with every inhale, exhale, and sacred *om*.

May you want for nothing because you already have everything.

May you be a testament to living (the large life or the modest), the map of a beautiful personal journey, amassing the nicks and scrapes that come from playing fiercely, loving wildly, and audaciously crossing over gusty seas.

May you find time for rest and recovery after you've blanketed the skies, or the battlelines, with your freak flag flying.

May the intentions you set be felt against the sides of mountains, ring into the ether, and settle in the bones of those not as fortunate as you.

And may those intentions keep us all connected like a mighty woven net of love that catches us always when we fall.

Happy living, all.

ENDNOTES

1. From *Anthem* by Leonard Cohen – pg 9
2. From *A Night Full of Talking* by Rumi – pg 9
3. *A Book of Silence* by Sara Maitland – pg 27
4. *Trees: An Anthology of Writings & Paintings* by Hermann Hesse – pg 56
5. Agape Spiritual Center teachings of Michael Bernard Beckwith – pg 76
6. From *Roderick Hudson* by Henry James – pg 82
7. From *The Big Book of Alcoholics Anonymous* by Bill W – pg 84
8. From *A Night Full of Talking* by Rumi – pg 84
9. From *Anthem* by Leonard Cohen – pg 91

ALSO BY ANGELA

BOOKS

Trading Fours *(novel)*
The Assassination of Gabriel Champion *(novel)*
Aleatory on the Radio *(100-word-story collection)*
Bones *(poetry collection)*
Viscera *(poetry chapbook)*
The Kidney Journals *(memoir)*
The Night, the City, and Miss Thing *(novelette)*

RECORDINGS

The Slow Club *(jazz)*
Expressionism *(jazz)*
Resting on the Rock *(alt folk)*
Music for the Weeping Woman *(alt folk)*
The Rainy Day Sessions *(jazz)*
Standard Procedure *(jazz)*
Winter *(holiday)*
Orphan Songs *(compilation)*
Angela *(pop fusion)*
Global Yoga *(wellness)*
Guided Meditations *(wellness)*

SHORT FILMS

The Richest Girl in the World *(illustrated film short)*
Six Murals *(documentary-short)*
The Sanctuary Project *(documentary-short)*
Occupy L.A. *(documentary-short)*
All These and More *(nod-to-bergman film short)*
Caught *(trance-poetic film short)*

Discover something new every day. Be in awe.

See treasures where others see nothing unusual.

From *The Goddess Project*

Born and raised in Los Angeles, now living and writing in Kansas City, Angela Carole Brown is the recipient of the 2018 North Street Book Prize in literary fiction for her novel *Trading Fours*, and Best Multimedia Film Awards from both the 2021 Buddha International Film Festival and the 2022 Indo Global International Film Festival for her film short *The Richest Girl in the World.* She is the author of several books in fiction, memoir, and poetry. She writes the blog Bindi Girl Chronicles, and has had shorter works and poetry published in *MacQueen's Quinterly*, *Flapper Press*, *Brilliant Corners*, *Thorny Locust*, *Echoes Media vMuseum*, and the poetry anthology *In the Black / In the Red*. She was on the L.A. music scene for nearly 40 years as a singer, songwriter, and recording artist, has produced several albums of music in the genres of jazz and folk, and for 28 years was the lead singer in Elvis Schoenberg's Orchestre Surreal before retiring from the profession in 2024. She is featured in the documentary film *The Goddess Project*. Though she has produced wellness CDs, *How the Light Gets In* marks Angela's first book in the genre.

LINKTR.EE/ANGELACAROLEBROWN

Made in the USA
Las Vegas, NV
29 April 2025

21485488R00066